T0380161

Going to school

Ephrem Mamo

This book is a work of non-fiction. Unless otherwise noted, the author and the publisher make no explicit guarantees as to the accuracy of the information contained in this book and in some cases, names of people and places have been altered to protect their privacy.

WestBow Press books may be ordered through booksellers or by contacting:

WestBow Press
A Division of Thomas Nelson & Zondervan
1663 Liberty Drive
Bloomington, IN 47403
www.westbowpress.com
1 (866) 928-1240

Because of the dynamic nature of the Internet, any web addresses or links contained in this book may have changed since publication and may no longer be valid. The views expressed in this work are solely those of the author and do not necessarily reflect the views of the publisher, and the publisher hereby disclaims any responsibility for them.

Any people depicted in stock imagery provided by Getty Images are models, and such images are being used for illustrative purposes only. Certain stock imagery © Getty Images.

ISBN: 978-1-9736-7136-7 (sc)
ISBN: 978-1-9736-7137-4 (e)

Library of Congress Control Number: 2019912041

Print information available on the last page.

WestBow Press rev. date: 8/29/2019

WESTBOW
P R E S S®
A DIVISION OF THOMAS NELSON
& ZONDERVAN

Enoch was born. He was excited to be part of his family.

Mommy and Daddy were excited to welcome Enoch.

When Enoch turned two years old, Mommy and Daddy decided to put him in school.

Enoch was scared to go to school. He would miss Mommy and Daddy.

Daddy replied, "I know, Son. We will miss you too. We will leave our picture with you, so whenever you miss us, you can look at the picture and remember that we love you."

The first day of school, Mommy and Daddy sat with Enoch for a while, read two books, and then said goodbye. Enoch felt excited about school.

Enoch met new friends and new teachers. He felt welcomed.

Enoch and his friends washed their hands
before they started their playtime.

Enoch and his new friends had so much fun playing together. Now, it was time to go potty. Teacher Nathan gave Enoch and his friends a two-minute warning before walking with them to the bathroom.

After Enoch and his friends went potty, they sat down for breakfast. Teacher Nathan, Amy, and Mia had a great conversation with them about their delicious breakfast.

The children ate their breakfast and cleaned up after themselves.

It was time to brush their teeth. Everyone had a blast.

After brushing their teeth, it was circle time. During circle time, the children sang the welcome song and talked about their feelings. Enoch is enjoying school.

Teacher Nathan told the children they were going outside. Enoch and his friends were extremely excited. Teacher Nathan told them about all the toys that were on the playground: bikes, balls, a sandbox, and sand toys.

Enoch was having a wonderful day, but after lunch, he began to miss his parents. He remembered that Mommy and Daddy had left him their family picture. It was almost naptime, so Enoch grabbed the picture and sat on his mat.

Mary said, "I am tired."

"Great job sharing your feelings, Mary," Teacher Amy said. "You did a lot today. You went to the playground, ran around with your friends, played in the sandbox, kicked the ball a few times, and played on the balancing log."

Nick was angry because Mark had hit him. Nick screamed and made angry faces. Teacher Mia said, "It's okay to be angry, Nick, but we must use our words and tell a teacher what happened so they can help."

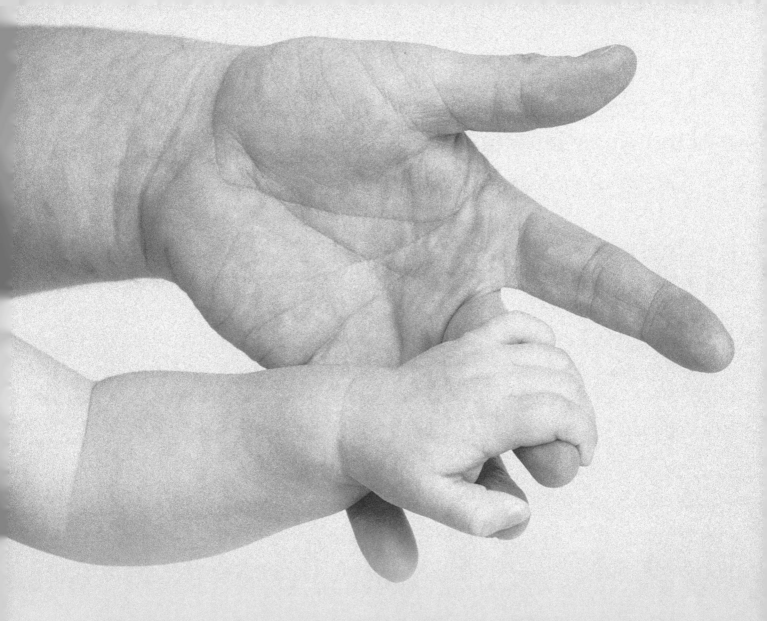

Teacher Amy talked to Mark next. "Mark, I know
you are frustrated, but instead of hitting, we need
to use words and practice gentle touch. When we
hit our friends, it hurts their bodies."

Luke was running in the classroom and fell and hurt his knee. Teacher Nathan said, "Luke, are you okay?" He helped Luke stand on his feet, and then he said, "Let's use walking feet, so we can be safe."

Matthew and Ruth told their friends to be quiet because it was naptime. Teacher Mia said, "Friends need to be quiet during naptime so that other friends can sleep."

Finally, Enoch and all his friends took a nap.

After naptime, Enoch and his friends went potty, had a snack, and enjoyed music and dancing.

Enoch wanted to sing "Twinkle, Twinkle, Little Star," and Teacher Mia said it was okay. Enoch and all his friends sang together and had fun.

Enoch and his friends sat down for storytime and read a story about a bee chasing her new friends, which was their favorite.

Enoch's parents arrived to pick him up. Enoch said goodbye to his new friends, and he knew that his friends would be just as delighted when their parents came to pick them up. Enoch felt scared about school at first, but now he could not wait to be back at school to his new friends and teachers.

Printed in the United States
By Bookmasters